FOREST BOOKS
FIRES OF THE SUNFLOWER

Ivan Davidkov was born on 9 March, 1926, in Zhivavtsi in the Mihailovgrad region of Bulgaria. His literary beginnings date from the '40s and '50s, but he soon became known as a fine lyric poet. He has written twenty volumes of poetry, but is also a distinguished novelist and artist. His literary awards have included the most prestigious given by the Bulgarian Writers' Union and the Soviet Writers' Union. This collection represents a selection of Davidkov's poetry from 1964 to 1988 and is illustrated by some of his own paintings.

Ewald Osers was born in Prague in 1917 but has lived in the United Kingdom since 1938. A writer and lecturer, he has translated over eighty books, twenty-one of them volumes of poetry. A fellow of the Royal Society of Literature, he has been awarded many prizes and in 1983 was given the Silver Pegasus of the Bulgarian Writers' Union.

FIRES
OF THE
SUNFLOWER

FIRES
OF THE
SUNFLOWER

Selected poems

of

IVAN DAVIDKOV

Translated from the Bulgarian

by

EWALD OSERS

FOREST BOOKS
LONDON ☆ BOSTON
1988

PUBLISHED BY
FOREST BOOKS

20 Forest View, Chingford, London E4 7AY, U.K.
P.O. Box 438, Wayland, MA 01788, U.S.A.

First published 1988

Typeset in Great Britain by Cover to Cover, Cambridge
Printed in Great Britain by A. Wheaton & Co Ltd, Exeter

British Library Cataloguing in Publication Data

Ivan Davidkov
Fires of the sunflower: selected poems
1. Osers, Ewald
891.8′113′08

ISBN 0 948259 48 5

Library of Congress Catalogue Card No 88–81866

Contents

Acknowledgements

Some of the poems in this volume have appeared in *Orbis* (Nuneaton, Warwickshire, U.K.), *Prospice* (Isle of Skye, Scotland, U.K.), *The Christian Science Monitor* (Boston, Mass., U.S.A.) and *Crosscurrents* (Westlake Village, California, U.S.A.)

Translator's Preface

Ivan Davidkov was born on 9 March 1926 in Zhivovtsi, in the Mihailovgrad region of Bulgaria. His literary beginings date from the turn of the forties and fifties, and he soon developed an individual profile as a lyric poet. His oeuvre now covers some twenty volumes of poetry. His first novel, 'Distant Fords', was written in 1967 and he has since published another eight works of prose. But whether writing poetry or prose, Davidkov is above all a meditative lyricist. These two elements – philosophical reflection and lyrical tone – are always closely related in his work, more especially in his recent books. They are related by subject, by reflection and by memories, which combine to present a colourful picture of life in a kind of dialogue about happiness, beauty, and the meaning of human existence. Characterized by a sense of detail and by a typical symbolism, their pictorial elements are drawn from nature. It would be difficult to separate Davidkov the prose writer from Davidkov the poet.

The present volume – the first to be published in English translation – represents a selection of Davidkov's work from 1964 to 1988, more particularly from his volumes *Hills under the Evening Star* (Хълмове под вечерницата1966), *Thracian Tumuli* (Тракийски могили 1968), *Illumination* (Озарение 1970), *Dance of Cypresses* (Танц на кипариси 1975), *Prayers for Chisel and Stone* (Молитви за длетото и камъка 1977), *The Ruler of Nocturnal Suns* (Владетелят на слънца нощните 1981), *Bird's Eye* (Око на птица1983), *Corrida* (Корида 1984), *The Departure of the Starlings* (Отлитането на скорците 1987) and *The Sea* (Морето 1988), with a deliberate weighting – as the author himself would wish it – towards the poetry of the past ten years. This more recent period shows an increasing shift of emphasis towards the philosophical component: generalization of human emotions and experience, reflections on human existence. Whereas his earlier poetry reflected a predominance of lyrical detail with no more than a philosophical sub-text, Davidkov's more recent work – especially *Corrida* – is characterized by philosophical reflection in lyrical language. The *leitmotif*, continually reappearing in a number of variations of his recent poetry (and indeed also of his latest prose writings) is the disturbing problem of the impermanence of human existence and

the problem of whether present-day man, both as an in-
dividual and as a species, will succeed in leaving behind
him a lasting mark of what is good and beautiful, and the
problem of whether man is still capable of active happiness.
These questions, of course, are as old as literature itself –
but the angle from which Davidkov views them is entirely
modern and topical. Davidkov's reflections on the core of
human existence are no arid philosophizing but an urgent
appeal to man to make every effort to save the spiritual
and material values which make human life beautiful and
meaningful, an appeal to man to fight evil, especially within
himself. And although many of his poems have a nostalgic
note, his poetry is ultimately not only profoundly human-
istic but also profoundly optimistic: the poet firmly believes
in the power of human friendship, in the invincibility of
noble sentiment and of the integrity of man ceaselessly
struggling against indifference and infamy, in man's
creative activity. The fundamental feature of Davidkov's
lyrical hero is humility, the exalted humility of a person
who has risen above pettiness. It is poetry without a pose,
without a striving for effect, poetry that has grown out of
life, out of suffering, into a purity of form, into genuine
unity of form and content.

Ivan Davidkov is not only a writer and a poet but also a
painter of some distinction – a fact that emerges from his
diction, no matter whether he writes philosophically reflec-
tive poems, or love lyrics, or playfully aphoristic short
poems suggestive of miniature paintings. His images are
drawn mainly from nature, which he knows and loves inti-
mately – which is why he has sometimes, but quite wrongly,
been described as a nature poet. He draws his principal
inspiration from autumn, which fascinates him both by its
riot of colour and by the sadness of parting and dying. The
sensory image of Davidkov's world, however, does not
depend solely on his painter's eye for colour and compo-
sition but also on his sensitive ear for the magic of sounds.

A small selection of his poetry, moreover when trans-
posed into a very different linguistic and cultural tradition,
cannot hope to present an adequate picture of Davidkov's
lyrical talent in all its hues and shades. But it can at least
introduce to a readership still largely unacquainted with
Bulgarian literature a modern poet with deep reverence for
life, for its infinite and inexhaustible beauty, a sensitive
poet striving to be human in the best sense of the word.

Introduction
Flute Music Painted
on the Wall

The soul of the poet Ivan Davidkov is hidden in the
dust jackets of his books. This witty paradox becomes
clear when I add that for some twenty years all the
writer's books – poetry, prose, essays – have appeared in
his native country with dust jackets upon which are printed
reproductions of his paintings. Even though he is not a
professional artist, Davidkov is a very talented painter and
this fact appears even in the humble polygraphic repro-
ductions. The paradox, I repeat the word, is that the poet
revealed relatively late, at about the age of forty, the world
of colour, the spread of the singing shades.

As a pattern, the case is not surprising. The history of
world art knows a number of cases of the talented co-
habitation of poet and artist in one and the same person-
ality. It is enough to recall the names of Michelangelo and
Blake. And many know of the passion of Goethe, Hugo and
Pushkin for representational art.

Ivan Davidkov's painting (his favourite genre is land-
scape painted in oils) is an alternative expression to poetry.
When he is not writing, the poet likes to paint, and vice
versa. But with him the link between the two arts is much
deeper, more real. His lyric is colour-impressionistic, while
his painting is pastel-lyric, as though the poet flees to the
word and the palette so as to express one and the same
sacred truth. What is that?

True poetry is difficult to subject to interpretation. The
connotational halo of the words and their combinations
presupposes many more meanings and points of departure
than criticism can observe. And we must not forget some-
thing else – that, in the etymological sense of the word, the
lyric is a song, that is that it is subject to the magic of the
incantational, the sung word.

All this there is in Davidkov. There is the musical virtu-
osity of the mastered word, there is the tinted whirlwind of
image-associations, there are the depths of philosophical
penetration into the meaning of the insoluble riddle, which
is life. Davidkov is one of the most recognisable of contem-

porary Bulgarian poets, a creator with his own lyrical style and presence in current Bulgarian literature.

Ivan Davidkov's life, at first glance, offers no dramatic events or experiences. Born in 1926 in the village of Zhivovtsi in northwestern Bulgaria (it no longer exists, having been drowned some ten years ago by the waters of the reservoir near Mihailovgrad) the talented young man began to write while he was still at school; his verse was noticed, and soon after the war he was invited to edit the children's newspaper *Septemvriiche*, where he was lucky enough to work for some time with Elin Pelin, one of the classics of Bulgarian literature. It is worth noting from these years of his youth, his one-year stay in Kiev, where he was sent to learn Ukrainian and to get acquainted with the related slavonic literature. It was hardly a coincidence that his first collection of verse, *The Ukrainian with the White Harmonica* (1951) contains the stamp of this contact with Ukrainian poetry.

For long years, until he retired in 1986, Davidkov worked as Editor-in-chief of one of the most prestigious publishers – 'Bulgarski pisatel'. He received literary awards – the leading award of the Union of Bulgarian Writers, and the highest literary award of Soviet Ukraine. But his life was free of vivid external events because perhaps as with every notable creative writer, his real life was the life of the spirit. His spiritual biography is contained in his books. Reading them, we can follow the turns of his ever-searching thought, the doubts and self-rejections of the creative artist.

Ivan Davidkov is a fruitful writer. The total of his titles must be approaching forty, among which are numbered some ten novels. It would take much space even to list the titles of his collections of verse, and so I shall content myself with mentioning only those published during the last few years: *The Eye of a Bird* (1983), *Corrida* (1984), *The Flight of the Starlings* (1987), and *The Sea* (1988). These books are worthy of attention not only because they are the most recent to be published, but also because they find a place among the most mature in the already numerous works of Davidkov.

It is very difficult to generalise about the nature and the unique magic of Ivan Davidkov's poetry in a few lines. This is even more difficult when selected extracts of that poetry are rendered into a foreign language. I have already read two of the poet's works in a translation by Ewald Osers in an American anthology of contemporary world poetry, and I am convinced that the unique impression of his lyric will get through to the English-speaking reader. I consider the attraction of Davidkov's verse lies in the special combination of balladic concentration of feeling and the vivid colourful imagery, unlocking numerous associations. The poet's imagery has a special, unique character. The many images in his verse – landscape, to do with things – are built upon the principle of metaphorical dematerialisation and disembodiment of the image. Spiritual and physical, material-bodily and intellectual, continually flow together and change places in the colour-impressionistic amalgam of this poetry. From this maybe comes the feeling of a deeply pantheistic sense of the world of the poet, for whom life is without end in the sense of a boundless spiritualisation of 'dead' nature through the presence of man.

Davidkov's poetry is more magic than his painting. If we try to put some of his poems upon canvas, there will shine from them some of the visions of Marc Chagal. Judge for yourselves – in the poem 'Crocus' (from the collection *Corrida*) the poet fixes two images, linked metaphorically with spring and hinted at in the title: of the horse which turns the wheel of the water pump, and of the ploughman walking after his plough. Both images are 'dematerialised' through symbolic-metaphorical constructions, which recall the 'ghostly landscapes' of the Symbolists. Thus, for example, the horse which circles 'winds up time itself, as it were.' And again, the sun will return to the world 'when the bucket from the well pours out its dreams'. The ploughman's plough, again, strikes not into the earth, but into 'the cawing of rooks' and 'their flocks rise with a slap – as if they are leaves from a silent apple-orchard.'

Above all this, in the mature poetry of Davidkov, hovers the halo of an unconquerable nostalgia, arising from the consciousness of the brevity and unrepeatability of human life. The poet is aware, as it were, that he is drawing with frozen breath upon heavenly silk, that what is created by man is impermanent and precisely for that reason is so tragically sublime. He is not consoled by faith in the deathlessness of the word which remains. But in truth it remains as a sign of the unrepeatability of man, as a scar on the bark of the thousand-year-old tree of poetry, as a bitter triumph of the unrepeatable human spirit, which never wearies of seeking a way through the flumes of the merciless mill of time.

With these characteristics in his poetry, Ivan Davidkov is not only a Bulgarian but also a world poet. I am convinced that his verse will encounter a response among English-speaking readers also, and this will be a further affirmation that culture is worldwide property, that in our days the frontiers cease to be geo-political phenomena but will pass through human hearts and particularly through the capacity of man for love and understanding.

Simeon Hadjikosev
Lecturer in Western European Literature at
the University of Sofia and Deputy President
of the Institute of Literature at the
Bulgarian Academy of Sciences.

The Poems

My eyes are full of misty distances

Don't look for me. For I have long
departed. And your letters are not likely
to find me. Rocky gorges
follow me with their flowering dogwood trees.
And quarries provide marble
on which to sit. There, opposite
the corrugated iron sheds, rust-red
from rain, I listen to the
ring of the chisel. As the stone extends
its arms and lips in order to enjoy —
a million years from now – the sky
and the green fields. Silent, I hear
the voice of mystery – and I walk away
like a dislodged stone rolling down the slope.
What have I gained over these past few days?
Dust on my shoes, one single poem
of clay and clouds, one dry piece of bread,
a witness to my sleepless nights
and the mad resurrection of the marble
and of my soul under the chisel's edge.

My staff converses with the road.
My eyes are full of misty distances.

Spring

The bursting of the cherry buds awoke me,
made tenfold by the echo of the morning.
And cheerfully the front latch clicked.
Was it the spring day
that had tried to open
my door?

I went outside.
The south wind, with a throat gone hoarse,
was talking to the trees bent to the ground,
and a child's kite,
flown out of someone's dream,
danced like a feather ahead of me.

A song was being born
of countless roads
and the black ploughland
turned golden with seed.

Two hills
with invisible hands
rocked a silver line
on the horizon.

And it rose
smoothly, rhythmically,
touching a cloud,
then a young girl
resembling you
hopped underneath it
on one leg.

Пролет

Събуди ме пукот на пъпки черешови,
от ехото на утрото удесеторен.
И весело тракна резето. —
Не беше ли
открехнал вратата ми
пролетният ден?

Излязох.
Южнякът със гърло пресипнало
говореше на дърветата, до земята
                              приведени,
и детско хвърчило,
из нечий сън излитнало,
се мяташе като перушинка напреде ми.

Раждаше се песен
на пътища неизброими
и ставаше златна от семе
черната оран.

Два хълма
със своите ръце незрими
люлееха сребърното въже
на кръгозора.

И то се издигаше
плавно, ритмично,
докосваше облак,
после — дръвче,
и някакво момиченце,
на тебе прилично,
подскачаше под него
на едно краче.

The Mirror

The mirror is an abyss. In it
images quietly sink
without our hearing a sound, without our seeing
the rippling of running waves.
There, on the bottom, lies hidden
the secret soul of our house,
where we are born, where others sometimes
lived before us.

No matter whether we cry or pray,
they won't float up again
out of the wordless depth.
And cracked by our wrinkles,
silvery like the morning mist,
the mirror keeps its silence.

There was an artist once

There was an artist once. A little eccentric.
That's what the grown-ups said. But we children
curiously followed him about
and watched him
swaying under the load of his canvases.

His stopping place was where
the waves of hills were rising.
His easel anchored him
to this big world
and a lark's song
was his advisor.

Bare-chested ploughmen moved across the field,
the horses hot, the reins all taut,
and he repeated their furrows
with the clouds in the sky
and sowed stars in them.

And he, wrapped in his threadbare scarf,
the echo of the skylark's song now done,
called on the trees, half-closed his eyes —
and they sank roots into his canvas.

On his return he scarcely moved,
his steps becoming one
with the steps of the barefoot.
Was it so easy then
to carry so many hills and clouds
under his arm?

In winter his little window was a murky patch.
And when outside he heard the blizzard raging
he'd light one sun upon his canvas
so it should warm not just his hands, but the trees.
Where had he got it from? The angry sky?
No, that is black, an icy wind is dropping its needles.
He must have carried it hidden in his cap,
the way young boys do a fledgling sparrow
that's fallen from its nest.

Such people leave nothing behind —
they give joy to others and themselves live on bread.
And as they die they light a fire so great
that future days will sit by it
and warm themselves.

They do not gather tiny crumbs
for their contentment,
they live in sleeplessness
and wordlessly they die,
abandoning galaxies of sentiment and sun.

Practical people
find it hard to understand them.

Sonnet

I come to recreate you all new,
give greater range to your ideas' flights,
and for your steps horizons to pursue,
and brilliant moonlight to your sleepless nights.

I come, triumphant and in some alarm,
to help you from your daily toil to rise,
make up a marriage bed to keep us warm,
with calls from heaven and with children's cries.

For thus I shall ensure that you live longer:
transporting past oblivion and decay
your tears and laughter also — and despite

being an invented god, whose prayer strongly
breathes life into your earthen-coloured clay
and vanishes in silence in its night.

The return of the storks

1.

The storks arrived at early dawn
over our valley
not yet warmed by the sun.
From the purple Berkovitsa hills
the light was pouring
on their enormous flock.

The windows of the houses shone like fire.
People awoke and stepped outside
to see if they could recognize their storks.
Were they the same?
Even the telephone wires sang from joy.

The flock was in no hurry. The beat of their wings
mingled with
the whisper of the peach buds.
Wherever they spotted a village in the valley
they'd circle it three times
slowly and solemnly.

Three silver wreaths of wings
interweaving
above smiles,
above poplars,
above white paths —
and then two storks flew down,
they'd found their old nest.

And the flock carried their light away
to other villages and other joy —
and once again above the stony hills
three silver rings were woven.

And cap in hand
the people stood,
leaning on their ploughs,
leaning against young trees.
Until that day you'd never seen them
so radiant, so inspired.

The morning had entranced them with a magic
which lent their souls a splendour of their own.
The valley silently observed a liturgy
that no religious creed had ever known.

2.

From Ogosta to Kom
no plough that morning will break the clods,
the unsown seed
will sprout on the man's palm,
but still they stood, heads bared, before that beauty,
but still they stood, heads bared, before the loyalty
of these big red-beaked birds.

So many wide seas had they crossed —
they had not stayed among the dunes of the Nile,
and their flock's cloud
was scattering above the Danube's fields.

They had returned here —
to the rimless wheel
placed on the roof
of the old water-mill,
to the clang of the blacksmith,
to the garden with its lilies,
to the airy kites
of the village children.

The others have passed by. Far away. Far away.
No doubt over the Danube now they're drawing
three silver circles —
so small that they resemble
the pupil of a
small child's eye.

The bitter smoke . . .

The bitter smoke of burning leaves is rising.
It's cold. What shall I throw round your shoulders?
Your brightly-coloured shawl, knitted of summer's rain-spouts?
Or of the sound of vanishing flocks of sheep?

Caravans of stars carry our night thoughts towards the sky,
but we remain within our horizon's confines.
And the larks on the rutted track
peck their last song.

Echo

Who called you to this world and who directed
your eyes to joy and emptiness?

Hope led me. I could see its words
up in the sky. They were like birds
which landed in the hoof-marks of the horses
and in the dust of those who came before me.

Where did you leave your happiest day?
And could you resurrect it with your cry?

I left it at the bottom of my bitterest tear
like a fly trapped in ancient amber
and there it rests, enormous and enchained
by the faint echo of my feeble cry.

And have you kept your former halo bright,
like on a fresco down which runs the rain?

I've saved the sacredness of fire. And I hope
my final hour will be sacred. Let it wear
a halo from the lamp of a nocturnal pilgrim —
and let the others think it is my crown of thorns.

15

Little night music

Will anyone be coming
with love to cure my pain?

A ladies' band is strumming
on the Boulevard Saint-Germain.

Old tunes, but still enchanting,
Italian, sad and gay,
as of the Trevi fountain
jets of a long-past day.
Beyond the white hill's corner
the pines are on the march,
seeking the road to Livorno
under the night's dark arch.
Ancient capriccios are pounding
their musical feet again,
thinly the trumpets are sounding —
why do they give me such pain?

A kingdom for Rome or Milano,
for a southern sunrise and set!
Parla italiano?
Non, madame . . . je regrette . . .

I see: round the white hill's corner
the pines are on the march,
seeking the road to Livorno
under the night's dark arch.
Or are they possibly coming
to spend the night with my pain?

The Italian ladies are strumming
on the Boulevard Saint-Germain.

Prelude and Fugue

Prelude and fugue heard under the stained glass of Notre-Dame.
The evening rain running down the cold forest of stone colonnades:
was it the organ's voice that drove me like a startled sparrow
into their leafless branches,
or was it just a dream?

The sunset's fading on the stained-glass windows
and evening's setting out in its black coat past the shop-fronts of
St. Germain-des-Prés.

Oh, spare my eyes, sounds falling like slow autumnal leaves!

Prayers, like steam from railway stations, slow and pungent,
                                                    rise to heaven,
and through their mist I see the faces of stone saints
resurrected by music:
with their immortality, as though with a handkerchief,
                                        they wipe their foreheads,

they smile, they bow to one another
until their haloes touch with metallic ring,
their God-given haloes so alike to those
handed out on earth for obedience and unfaltering faith.

Alone with a black halo, painted by a rising lark,
stands a railwayman from Rambouillet . . .
I'm chilly here among these walls of stone.
With hands outstretched, like a blind man, I'll grope my way
                                                    to the exit,
to let the bridges' wings, heavy with dusk and mist,
carry me up into the grey Paris morning.

2.

I think I'll live to hear the first bee's song,
the gentle explosion of the trees in blossom,
and some white cloud will take my soul by the hand
after these wintry mists,
which for so many months have painted on my windows
illusive trees and echoless wide plains.

I'll come, a wedding guest, to white-robed waterfalls
and to you, peach-trees,
blooming on southern slopes.
I'll come and see your bows and ribbons
untied by swallows and the vernal wind.

The dew will tie a brotherly bond between
my fleeting face
and the eternity of the sun which rises
above hill-tops.

The dew will teach me to rise from the dead, just as it does itself,
spring after spring.

3.

I'm standing at the end of a smile as on a sheer cliff.
Below lie all the seas that I have crossed.
In the far distance I can see the sirens' islands
and the masts of the ship where the ropes
are assuaged longings that cut deep into my flesh.

Then the sunsets strode the shores like lions.

Now I stand in the dusty grass,
a captive to my memories of the waves' white cords,
engraved on my palms the seagulls' cries.

Day breaks. Above me, like a violin,
the window swinging in the wind is singing.
Beyond it I see women I have loved.
Softly they float among my dreams, as if afraid
to shed the golden pollen of men's caresses
from off their shoulders and their faithless hearts.

And in my dream that night galloped the horses of my days —
bursting through the fence of sunlight,
erected in the puddles along the road to the Universe —
and under the hooves remained my thoughts and loves
like trampled grass . . .

Bell towers, for whom is your morning prayer?
For absolution of the exulting sinful flesh?
Or is it a benediction of the unborn —
      that golden little fish in its mother's womb,
which will set forth into the streams of life,
into the invisible fish-net of death that lies in wait . . .

I'm standing at the end of a smile as on a sheer cliff.
Below lie all the seas that I have crossed.
And on the rocks I see the waves' reflections,
and I believe they are the morning's angels
preening the golden feathers of their wings
of the soot of our chimneys . . .

4.

At an age when people are getting old
and wall themselves in among furniture and memories
                                        I began to open
forgotten books of children's fairy-tales.

Tin soldiers on parade
are presenting arms to the midnight hour
and a fair-haired boy
from the tale of the Emperor's new clothes
propped on his elbows in my dream
calls out: 'Heh look, the Emperor's got no clothes on!'

The procession passes under my window —
and I can see you, doomed to serve the word.
The footmen dip their quills
like spears and in their solemn hands they hold
your exquisite attire, woven of
the finest silk of words and flattery.

Your brow, for which the bronze is kept in readiness,
glistens under its slender laurel wreath.
Your step is confident, triumphant,
through flanking crowds. But that small boy is laughing
and in his laughter all the golden
cloaks turn to dust. And now I see you
grey as a plaster cast,
and in my ears still ring the winds
beneath the laurel, wisely silent.

The child shouts: 'Look, the Emperor's got no clothes on!'
I listen to your voice and, startled, wonder
if I've gone blind or if I'm seeing phantoms,
because I'm seeing with my soul . . .

But they will tell me I am gravely ill.

5.

Some day I'd like to say to my typewriter: 'Thank you
for teaching me with the song of your keys
and with the song of rain to buy
a bitter mouthful. Stay until I have
a pile of my own books. Then you can rest.'

I was a travelling hawker of songs.
I bartered my strolls about the sky for everyday things
and my golden dreams were thought worth a few coins.
I'd like to go and find a harbour.
Meet the first steamships with their shawls of seagulls
and with a rope tossed over from aboard
like a fraternal handshake.
Or, lying in a mountain meadow, watch the birds.
And for my songs the evening shall give me bright stars
on the bottom of every pool — at the hour when
the quarrymen return.

I'd like to earn my bread with hands calloused
from wielding pick-axe
or chisel, to let the pupil of the eye
read from the veins on the marble's hand
the ancient mysteries of the earth.

I'd like a slow, enormous moon to rise
over my conscience and the quiet valley . . .

6.

I have received your letter from Babylon —
and as the lizards darted
before you over the fragments of granite and glory,
so do my eyes now dart about the roughnesses
of words.

I'm climbing up into the empty sky
by the ladder of birds' voices.
Where is the tower of Babel now?
Who'll tie the mad multiplicity of tongues
        into a vipers' knot
to sow from the peaks of glory
thistle and scorpion?

Like a nomadic horde sand follows our tracks.
The horses fence us in with tossing manes.
They have no riders. Only the wind
flings from the sky their memory, like a black mantle,
and their teeth grind the dead grass of sounds
from the bare wasteland.

Where is the tower of Babel now?
Answer me, distant voices, tied in a viper's knot!

The thistle is silent, like a beggar it has set out
                                from among the ruins.

Perhaps I'll try to fly,
but my wings will be heavy
from the dust of cares and doubts,
and alongside me, in the sand, my feathers will mark out a trail
in which the vipers settle for the night.

7.

Painting perhaps is madness. But my house smells
of paint that hasn't yet dried. And I bless you,
wild fever of my soul. Canvases — white plains —
record the brush's steps, like footsteps of a sower,
and a quail streaks up from a leaden tube.

Who'll teach me to look for you, moments of miracles?

One airman — in retirement — kept bees
and every morning came to listen to
the hives awakening. Their hum reminded him of airfields
abandoned in remote parts of the world. And over the
old airman's features flickered soundlessly
the gleam of aircraft taking off.

But that was in my childhood. The man I walked with
no longer had wings
and I was humming like a tree in blossom,
captured by his miracle.

Now, left behind in the mists, I pray:
'Save me, my visions of the morrow,
let not the puddles chain my legs
with rain's rusty fetters . . .'

And I feel saved anew.

The paints exude the smell of healing herbs and quays.
And ports with bent-back dockers come to eat
at my house. And my brush, like a sparrow, pecks at the crumbs
that have dropped on the worn carpet.

Sunday solemnities of my soul,
my hard and jubilant day, and also my prison,
At nightfall I return to the hut of my brief dreams
and like a prison warder,
leaden-eyed, spy through the keyhole
tomorrow's troubles.

8.

Cardiologists, can you hear the groan of the trees,
the arhythmia of awakened waterfalls
and the feverish heart-beat in the hooves of maddened
                                                    horses?

How deep your reins have bitten into us, alarming time!
The Rider's back is glossy with sweat and his muscles
jerk feverishly with a breathless pulse
like grass in the wind.

Shall we fall off before we've gnawed through the reins?

The heart drops its thick beats like boulders tumbling down
the steep slides of a quarry.

Perhaps this is an infernal machine in the earth's heart,
which with resounding rattle —
just like the alarm clock on my shelf at home
in those autumnal days of my far-off childhood —
now inexorably counts down
the minutes, along whose fuse
with its red ants horror will creep —
and our last breath will shrivel up
like a charred root . . .

9.

I'll go and see the chestnut trees in bloom
along the banks of the Berkovitsa,
their blossom-spikes like starfish on the coast of Brittany
lie, mother-of-pearl-like, on the sea-wet meadows
when winter's floods receded but its spume still gleams
along the mountain ridges.

I'll take a few favourite books and pictures.
And in the evening I'll invite the west,
      he'll sit down by the door —
the only guest — when fires will flare up.
And when loneliness comes I will call the fireflies
at midnight in July — the most delicate ballerinas —
      to come and dance for me,
and silently I'll say my goodbyes to them
and no one in the darkness shall
observe my farewell tear.

If you remember me send me a letter
without protestation of friendship — simply write
two or three ordinary words. I'll be so pleased
if a small blackbird knocks upon my door
carrying a letter in a writing I remember.

And like a diver I shall then set out to seek the starfish
on the bottom of
the silence under the chestnuts by the Berkovitsa.

In time you will be . . .

In time you will be just a memory,
city of nightfall. Japanese cherries
will shed their blossom, and the blackbird's song
will mingle with the smoke of sleepy stations
deep in the snow's embrace. And I shall watch
through the dim window of the railway car
my thoughts going out to find you,
their nacrous footsteps
crisscrossing windy platforms
and filling up with emptiness and dusk.

And on the Scheldt the steamboats will be plying
and ploughing up the bare expanse,
so rain and seagulls plant their seeds in them.
And bays will shimmer grey with emptiness
just like my heart — no echo of
sail-canvas, no reflection.
One spot of shade alone is left to me,
rocking among the oil slicks on the water,
a crumpled newspaper ripped up by
        the fingers of the north wind.

Antwerp, 1977

Adagio

The fires of the sunflower fields are dead.
Crows are the black charcoal with which autumn draws
the portrait of the rain on barren limestone cliffs.
The grass is trying in its cold embrace to keep the wind
                                                on its bed,
but the wind angrily throws off its rust-coloured blanket.
And the song of grasshoppers in the fields is so dry
that it falls like ash upon your eye-lids.

Tell me, how many steps are left to you
        from the delicate cherry blossom
to the silent titmouse in the bare branches?

If you attempt to heat your house with thoughts
you'll hear the ice tinkling in your kettle.
If you attempt to light the walls with memories of sunshine
you'll see the spider's dream gently rocking
in all the corners. Clouds will walk
along the words you've written
between the blackbird's voice and the banshee's
        howling over the chimney.

Tell me, your clothes for the awaited feats, have the moths
                                been at them
or is it starlight I can see?

Distances whistle in the leafless poplar branches.
The soul seeks feast-days so it can believe it is immortal.
The soul sends out its cares to play, like children,
about the circuses, the fairground shooting galleries,
and it puts on new clothes still redolent of moth-balls,
cheerfully reaching for the cup the Lord has filled,
not noticing his cold and piercing eyes.

Tell me, if I attend the celebration — as an acrobat —
                        along the white trail of the plane,

shall I then find the hope which I had dropped into
                                the abyss of the setting sun?

Thus with the crows' hoarse cry the autumn draws
the portrait of rain on barren limestone cliffs.

Meteor

1.

Before you can cry 'Stop!' — you're falling on your back
and across your eyes a horse will flash
with huge flanks — like a forest
aflame when leaves are falling. You'll see
the reins — two ropes stretched
between sky and earth, up which
with lips pressed tightly you can climb
above your pain, breaking loose like a nail
from the dry soil into which your final hour
has driven you. But your hands will touch
only the tired snorting of the stallion,
the wind, the silvery light
of the first star. The unenduring friendship
of those last moments will get frayed — and you will fall
downward — into yourself — and you'll pierce that
                                        bottomless infinity
like a huge black meteor.

Your soul will set out on tiptoe —
so as not to wake your sleeping body —
and your last cry will flesh out like a knife
thrust into the sky's ribs.

2.

At the tormenting hour *She* will come to mould
our faces out of clay and out of ash.
And streams of rain will wash our eyebrows, eyes and lips —
and we'll resemble roadside stones
or clods of earth turned over by the plough.

Where are the rotting bones of our words?

That tree in bloom, why is it hovering
                              over that bare hill —
is it not searching for their traces?
And that bird-hunter with his snare, why is he tracking it
as if it were a bird?

3.

When truth puts on its white clothes on the grass
and sinks into the embraces of the devil —
our thoughts will turn to soot
and from their flour we'll knead our bread.
The fire will turn away from me
and dance like mad over the roof.
In the most pink-cheeked word of the child
a worm will settle as if in an apple
and wind will sweep across the fields,
wearing a cloak of desert sand.

4.

Therefore I say to the blossoming tree: 'Live,
to let the magic of the miracle live!
Live like the stone-cutter who has emerged
from winter's hell and lifts his eyes to heaven.
Live, dressed by birds' wings,
by the speech of all springs, by the rhythm of all steps
reminding us of the breathing of the Universe!

If we are very poor at our final hour
lend us your shirt that we may leave with it
from here. And you move on across the naked field
and wait for the resurrection of the light.

Before the infinite vastness swallows us we'll sit upon the hill
and I shall see you flow along like foam
down the wild reins of the galloping horse.

And lightning will be flashing in the sky,
and hills will crack asunder
from distant whinnying.

And with the horse comes *She* who bears not fame
                                    but retribution . . .'

The clown

In memory of Tsvetan

1.

If I inquired where the clown has gone who'd answer me?
The rain? The vanishing shadow of the tram?
                              Or else the butterfly
up in the sky above the peeling buildings?
And who will walk towards me clumsily,
his coat unbuttoned and his tie askew —
the poplar by his home or the budding lilac?
And if they wish to tell me something in his voice,
                              will I then understand
their words or will they be drowned
by the voice of the woodworm that is now my companion?

2.

From youth he roamed the fairs
with wandering showmen: acrobats and fakirs. He would be
a target for knife-throwers
who with their whistling blades outlined
his portrait on boarded walls.
From these wanderings he retained
a sense of the magic of fire:
it drew his close, the way a candle attracts a moth.
I used to see him on cool August nights
lighting the flames and then dancing in it
held in a fire-dancer's trance.
He used to come to our home on saints' days.
And as the glasses rose like a flock of red birds
he did his favourite magic trick; he struck a match
and we then watched the flames come from his nostrils.
And on the wall I watched the bacchanale of shadows:
it seemed to me that in the dusty grass
men with long gypsy knives were slicing
huge fiery resonant melons.
But what I could not understand was why
he tried so hard to tame the all-consuming fire,
make it his friend — the self-same fire
which before long would strike him down
on crumpled bed-sheets, on a pillow
which bears the imprint of his waxen face.

3.

He ran at midnight to inform me that
the swallows had returned that evening,
the peach-tree by his window was in blossom
and its bright light stopped him from falling asleep.
But no one rang at the hour when he walked
the narrow tight-rope of his final breath
and when below his feet he clearly felt
not the brilliant vastness of the circus ring
but the infernal abyss in the eyes of those
whom he was leaving behind.

Yes, clowns know how to die with a smile,
dress up the ring's silence
in their most colourful costumes,
smile at the lions growling at their tamer,
smile at the gold braid and at the whip
which makes even conscience stand on its hind-legs.
They know they are not saying goodbye to the circus,
but their future ring is a hypocritical smile
an obsequious word, and a hand in a hurry
to open the door to the boss.
Yes, clowns have the keys to our own homes
and we may see them unexpectedly
as we remove an overcoat in the hall
and turn towards the mirror.
They gaze at us from a bottomless glassy depth,
a smile round their sad eyes in which the entire firmament
                                        trembles
like some gigantic tear ready to drop into our soul, to startle us
with the din of the big, faded, dusty top.

Quite suddenly . . .

Quite suddenly I treasure like a miser
those fleeting moments I once squandered so heedlessly,
entrapped by the temptations of youth.

I see that in my hand there now remains
but little sand of life's vast fine-grained dune
which once I thought could never trickle through my
                                        fingers —
and now I watch each grain
like that entire big world which I am leaving.

My thoughts are getting tired, I can sense it.
My words are crouching, dusty, by my feet.
And yet my eyes, with childlike curiosity, still seek
                        the mysteries of existence —
and it seems to me that only now do I understand
                        the lark's morning prayer
and on which saint's day the butterflies
                        perform their formal dance.

The fallen apples tell me: 'Autumn's coming . . .'
Bridges beckon me to a walk
and distant hills, taking my breath away, attempt
like rain-soaked birds to soar into infinity
on wings of lightning.

And now I understand the secret magic
of contemplation, which I had
always resisted so as to leave room
for impulses and passions. Now
I'm like the earth which has known seed
and flowering and hail and now reposes
under a slow autumnal sun,
thoughtful and weary,
a single flower by the field's edge, where now
a bee is buzzing and a ploughman harnesses
his horse — and a cheerful furrow
steams when the ploughshare's passed, red as a sunrise.

The negress

I expected the black girl dancer to flare up like coal
in the rhythm of jazz,
but only the ash of African fires
gleamed silvery in her eyes.
Behind her, like a tiger, crept a long shadow
through the jungle of her wild movements
and I could hear the swish of the lianas
at the sudden leap of the startled gazelle.

Pastoral

Far from the dusty quarry,
far from the midday rush,
women undress on the bank
and shyly step into the river.

They expect a gentle caress from the waves,
but instead the current fiercely grabs them
with a man's hands, pressing them close,
choking with slippery coolness
against shoulders and thighs. They resist,
angrily but laughing, they don't see
that in the willow's foliage
a snow-white butterfly peeps at them
like a boy's enraptured eye.

And they abandon themselves to the stream's hands
with yielding body and with misted eye.

Then

I want to tell you something very tender . . .

Then I'll sit down and turn the pages
of the clouds' notebook, so as to read
the swallows' love sonnet, written with
the ink of their delicate wings
and the grass's fragrance.

And my lamp at night will be the apple-tree in blossom.

Bird's eye

1.

Some day we'll become attendants in the Garden of Eden
— unless the job has gone to one of God's relations —
or else (and far more likely) we shall toil, sleepless, in the
quarries of Hell
while the sun moves round the hill with the watchful eyes
of a prison guard.

Is this the promise you're holding out to us, heaven?
You whose laughter was in the dew under childish sandals,
you who in April walked this earth
dressed in fragrant lilac?
And the sun, with whose golden laughter we wrote,
as if it were ink, in our copybooks,
why should it now be so merciless to us?
For what mysterious sin are we to be punished?
As children, when we woke, we saw on our pillows
its gossamer-like hair and felt its breath on our sleepy cheeks.
With it we went down to bathe in the river
and our clothes lay side by side in the sand:
ours old and patched, and the sun's all golden.
With it we climbed trees to go bird-nesting
and in its glances shimmered the silvery smoke of trains
that had passed . . .

Oh no, the sun will remain our companion!
Among the stars it will stride like a red-feathered cockerel,
singing at dawn in order to wake us
and through the rents in the clouds, God knows where,
we'll catch sight of
the road, smoke from a fire, a spring and a poplar
on whose bare top a chickadee is sitting.

And the stone will show mercy to our battered palms.

49

In the land of Copernicus . . .

In the land of Copernicus there lived an astronomer,
his hair as red as the sand of the Biblical deserts.
As a child, they said, he never had chicken-pox
but his face was pock-marked by falling stars,
for every night of his life he turned his eyes to the sky . . .

Where are the steps leading to his front door?
Why are you taking me to Auschwitz,
                          to the hall of artificial limbs?

He had no children: he adopted a little girl.
He called her by the starry name of Cassiopeia.
At night he'd bed her down in the Milky Way's blankets,
at dawn he'd wake her with the sunrise's tinkling —
even the alarm clock had a starry voice.

Where is that girl now? Why, in her little slippers,
is nothing left but a speck of cosmic dust?

He was an invalid. His wooden leg squeaked on his way
                          to death.
The sand of Biblical deserts rustled in his hair.
The flames engulfed him. And the smoke wrote on the
                          firmament
a quiet message to the stars.
And in his dust remained a tiny fragment of a
                          melted memory of Cassiopeia.

Now the wooden limb towers above the vast pile
                          of prostheses,
seeking a cloud for its ascension.

51

Clay and star

From the cycle of poems 'Clay and star'

1.

I sought my image in the looking glass
and my glance wandered over its rim,
anxious that it should not spin off
to its yawning whirlpools.
I saw reflected there the vast blue sky,
I saw the eyes, too, that were piercing it
and birds were flitting through the slits,
I saw the golden cloudlets — like those patches
on my short trousers many years ago —
and light was flashing from vast boundless meadows,
so clearly ready for the reaper's sickle.

This should have been my image?
Or did the looking glass invent my life?

Then with a tear I turned to her who stood by me.
I felt that I was hanging in the air — without support,
held by an opalescent tear and by
my innermost heart. I felt I was a captive,
not of the spark that glinted from the well of sorrow
but of the boundless ocean, where the evening rains
tread softly in their satin raiments.
And I discovered that my wrinkles are
                                    furrows under their feet,
that the rains come to sow in me
heavenly insight, that lightning will tread me in,
and that a silvery fish will plough me up,
ringing clear like an archangel's sword.

This should have been my image?
And could I, in my pain,
have hidden like a lizard in its furrow?

6.

I'll make myself a Trojan horse
from the pitch-covered planks of sunken ships,
from my grief over lost friends,
from memories of markets and of ports
which wound me with their jagged edges
like a splintered mosaic.

Inside its belly the Achaeans will be silent.

And as the gate of the doomed city opens
I'll realize that with our deceit we enter
not Troy, but that along my soul's streets
walk those to whom I'd given ringing spears and cunning —
and that those weapons are all aimed at me.

Against whom do I lead them? The doomed city
or against a phantom born of my own shout?
Who am I really — the Wooden Horse or Fear
that there is no one left with a swarthy skin to burst out free?

7.

This then was spring's goodbye to us?

I saw the gardener walking
among the flowering bushes, secateurs in hand.
A moment later the most beautiful rose
dropped under the merciless
                              steel,
its curly wig tumbling —
like the head
of Marie
      Antoinette
under the clank of the guillotine.

10.

See the cathedral of limetrees in blossom.
The high domes of amber,
the columns of fragrance, delicately sculpted
with the dawn's chisel,
and like a royal awning by the portal,
where the sun's rays will pass,
the melody of the early bees.

See the cathedral of limetrees in blossom.
This is a church for my heretical prayers,
where I go to hear the liturgy
of harvest, the golden hovering of its soul
over the river's current, over the watermill's wheel,
where the seed, like the Saviour, is doomed to suffer
in order to rise again
            in the white-toothed smile of broken bread.

See the cathedral of limetrees in blossom.
Listen to the bees' music,
in whose heaven the soul soars,
liberated and cleansed.
            Can this be
my victory over the deceptions
with which my nights and days surround me?
Redeemed by the bees' music
and raised to be god of the wandering clouds:
am I cleansed forever,
    or will the morning make me gullible?

See the cathedral of limetrees in blossom,
where the glow of the bees
burns my forehead.
    Of the Garden of Gethsemane I'll be reminded at midnight,
in my long sleepless night,
when the guards of darkness set out through the garden
and I am startled by the crowing of the cock.

56

That night

The summer day sky was like a bosom full of fireflies
that night when I loved you,
when we were holding hands,
and walking through the dark forest
seemed more like crossing a ford in heaven,
and underneath our feet, tottering, moved
Perseus and Andromeda —

where now
the laundered clouds are hanging
on the line strung up by a vanished aircraft
and only the yellowed grass
gives out sweet perfume to the sky
which — or was it just a dream? —
is like a bosom full of fireflights.

The first magnolia . . .

The first magnolia was out in the Ovcha Kupel gardens
and its shed blossoms
like large butterflies accompanied
the attendant
who swept the seats along the snowy drive.

A blue-tit sang. The popcorn in the kiosk by the bridge
scattered cherry blossom over the vendor's fingers
and the naked boy in the now thawing lake
felt how the fish he'd caught
flicked its brass tail
that snowy day
when the first magnolia was out in the Ovcha Kupel gardens.

Airfields in winter

Remember the airfields in winter
where your footsteps have now vanished
from the deserted runways — now
snow breathes there with whistling plumes.
Remember the pines along the highway
rising slowly and solemnly into the sky
like eagles over Fumicino.
Do their wings swish this night,
Does the guitar in the sailors' tavern
now lead the *horo* of the waves
or does the wet driftwood remind you
of the crickets' concert down near Naples?

Girl with white cap

I'm going to you. But how will you know
if I'm a cherry in bloom or a sapling in snow?

The way you embrace me will be my clue:
if a bee flies from my breath I shall know it's you.

Момичето с бялата шапка

— Вървя към тебе. Как ще разбереш
дали съм вишна цъфнала, или фиданка в скреж?

— Прегръдката ще ми подскаже. Ако излети
пчела над моя дъх, ще знам: това си ти. . .

If sometimes in the night

And nothing more . . .
V. Tkachenko

If sometimes in the night a late wind
awakes you and you hear my voice
like the deaf foghorn of a ship
lost in infinity,
know then that you have not set out alone
from the bare shore of your night:
I'm looking for you
just to hear your breath —
    and nothing more . . .

I've picked off all the ice-flowers
from the window — and in my vases they
now gleam like silver and like peacocks' tails,
waiting for you to come. Send me
a message by a bird, by a sunray flashing
through bare-branched poplars,
so I may believe that you exist,
you, distant one, you product of my mind —
    and nothing more . . .

65

Special Collection

THE NAKED MACHINE Selected poems of Matthías
Johannessen.
Translated from the *Icelandic* by Marshall Brement.
(Forest/Almenna bokáfélagid)
0 948259 44 2 cloth £7.95   0 948259 43 4 paper £5.95   96 pages
Illustrated

ON THE CUTTING EDGE Selected poems of Justo Jorge Padrón.
Translated from the *Spanish* by Louis Bourne.
0 948259 42 6 paper £7.95   176 pages

ROOM WITHOUT WALLS Selected poems of Bo Carpelan.
Translated from the *Swedish* by Anne Born.
0 948259 08 6 paper £6.95   144 pages. Illustrated

CALL YOURSELF ALIVE? The love poems of Nina Cassian.
Translated from the *Romanian* by Andrea Deletant and
Brenda Walker. Introduction by Fleur Adcock.
0 948259 38 8 paper £5.95.   96 pages. Illustrated

RUNNING TO THE SHROUDS Six sea stories of Konstantin
Stanyukovich.
Translated from the *Russian* by Neil Parsons.
0 948259 06 X paper £5.95   112 pages.

A VANISHING EMPTINESS Selected poems of Willem Roggeman.
Edited by Yann Lovelock.
Translated from the *Dutch*.
0 948259 51 5 £7.95   112 pages. Illustrated

PORTRAIT OF THE ARTIST AS AN ABOMINABLE SNOWMAN
Selected poems of Gabriel Rossenstock translated from the
Irish by Michael Hartnett. New Poems translated by
Jason Sommer.
Dual text with cassette.
0 948259 56 6 paper £7.95   112 pages

LAND AND PEACE Selected poems of Desmond Egan translated
into Irish by Michael Hartnett. Gabriel Rossenstock,
Douglas Sealey and Tomas MacSiomoin. Dual text.
0 948259 64 7 paper £7.95   112 pages

THE EYE IN THE MIRROR Selected poems of Takis Varvitsiotis.
Translated from the *Greek* by Kimon Friar. (Forest/Paratiritis)
0 948259 59 0 paper £8.95   160 pages

THE WORLD AS IF Selected poems of Uffe Harder.
Translated from the *Danish* by John F. Deane and Uffe Harder.
0 948259 76 0 paper £4.95   80 pages

THE TWELFTH MAN Selected poems of Iftighar Arif.
Translated from the *Urdu* by Brenda Walker and Iftighar Arif.
Dual text.
0 948259 49 3 paper £6.95   96 pages

SPRINGTIDES Selected poems of Pia Tafdrup.
Translated from the *Danish* by Anne Born.
0 948259 55 8 paper £6.95   96 pages

SNOW AND SUMMERS Selected poems of Solveig von Schoultz.
Translated from *Finland/Swedish* by Anne Born.
Introduction by Bo Carpelan. Arts Council funded.
0 948259 52 3 paper £7.95   128 pages

HEARTWORK Stories of Solveig von Schoultz.
Translated from *Finland/Swedish* by Marlaine Delargy and
Joan Tate. Introduction by Bo Carpelan.
0 948259 50 7 paper £7.95   128 pages

THICKHEAD AND OTHER STORIES Stories of Haldun Taner.
Translated from the *Turkish* by Geoffrey Lewis.
UNESCO collection of representative works.
0 948259 59 0 paper £8.95   176 pages

East European Series

FOOTPRINTS OF THE WIND Selected poems of Mateja Matevski.
Translated from the *Macedonian* by Ewald Osers.
Introduction by Robin Skelton. Arts Council funded.
0 948259 41 8 paper £6.95   96 pages. Illustrated

ARIADNE'S THREAD An anthology of contemporary Polish
women poets. Translated from the *Polish* by Susan Bassnett
and Piotr Kuhiwczak.
UNESCO collection of representative works.
0 948259 45 0 paper £6.95   96 pages

POETS OF BULGARIA An anthology of contemporary Bulgarian
poets. Edited by William Meredith. Introduction by
Alan Brownjohn.
0 948259 39 6 paper £6.95   112 pages

STOLEN FIRE Selected poems by Lyubomir Levchev.
Translated from the *Bulgarian* by Ewald Osers.
Introduction by John Balaban.
UNESCO collection of representative works.
0 948259 04 3 paper £5.95   112 pages. Illustrated

AN ANTHOLOGY OF CONTEMPORARY ROMANIAN POETRY
Translated by Andrea Deletant and Brenda Walker.
0 9509487 4 8 paper £5.00   112 pages.

GATES OF THE MOMENT Selected poems of Ion Stoica.
Translated from the *Romanian* by Brenda Walker and
Andrea Deletant. Dual text with cassette.
0 9509487 0 5 paper £5.00   126 pages
Cassette £3.50 plus VAT

SILENT VOICES An anthology of contemporary Romanian
women poets. Translated by Andrea Deletant and Brenda
Walker.
0 948259 03 5 paper £6.95   172 pages.

EXILE ON A PEPPERCORN Selected poems of Mircea Dinescu.
Translated from the *Romanian* by Andrea Deletant and
Brenda Walker.
0 948259 00 0 paper £5.95   96 pages. Illustrated

LET'S TALK ABOUT THE WEATHER Selected poems of Marin
Sorescu Translated from the *Romanian* by Andrea Deletant and
Brenda Walker.
0 9509487 8 0 papger £5.95   96 pages.

THE THIRST OF THE SALT MOUNTAIN Three plays by Marin Sorescu
(Jonah, The Verger, and the Matrix). Translated from the
Romanian by Andrea Deletant and Brenda Walker.
0 9509487 5 6 paper £6.95   124 pages. Illustrated

VLAD DRACULA THE IMPALER A play by Marin Sorescu.
Translated from the *Romanian* by Dennis Deletant.
0 948259 07 8 paper £6.95   112 pages. Illustrated

THE ROAD TO FREEDOM Poems and Prose Poems by Geo Milev.
Translated from the *Bulgarian* by Ewald Osers.
UNESCO collection of representative works.
0 948259 40 X paper £6.95   96 pages

IN CELEBRATION OF MIHAI EMINESCU Selected poems and
extracts translated from the *Romanian* by Brenda Walker and
Horia Florian Popescu. Illustrated by Sabin Balaşa.
0 948259 62 0 cloth £14.95   0 948259 63 9 paper £10.95   224 pages

THROUGH THE NEEDLE'S EYE Selected poems of Ion Miloş.
Translated from the *Romanian* by Brenda Walker and Ion
Miloş.
0 948259 61 2 paper £6.95   96 pages. Illustrated

YOUTH WITHOUT YOUTH and other Novellas by Mircea Eliade.
Edited and with an introduction by Matei Calinescu.
Translated from the *Romanian* by MacLinscott Ricketts.
0 948259 74 4 paper £12.95   328 pages

A WOMAN'S HEART Stories by Jordan Yovkov.
Translated from the *Bulgarian* by John Burnip.
0 948259 54 X paper £9.95   208 pages

Fun Series

JOUSTS OF APHRODITE Poems collected from the Greek
Anthology Book V. Translated from the *Greek* into modern
English by Michael Kelly.
0 948259 05 1 cloth £6.95   0 94825 34 5 paper £4.95
96 pages

Literary Review

The Literary Review, edited by Auberon Waugh and Laura
Cumming has tripled its circulation in twelve months but
is still almost unprocurable in many areas except by
subscription. A year's subscription costs only £15 and
secures twelve 64 page issues, printed on good glossy paper,
packed with reviews, competitions, book gossip, witty and
informed articles, pictures, cartoons, poetry and
occasional short stories. It is now essential reading for all
who wish to keep up with what is happening in the world
of letters – especially for those with insufficient time to
read everything.

I wish to subscribe to the Literary Review and enclose a cheque/
postal order for £15.00 (UK)/£20.00 (Europe)/£35.00 (Airmail
outside Europe)

Please debit my Access/VISA/American Express card number

Signature _____ Date card expires _____

Name _____

Address _____

_____

_____ Post Code _____

LITERARY REVIEW 51 BEAK STREET LONDON W1R 3LF

Forest Books publications are reviewed in
the *Literary Review*